WILD BABIES

MARGRIET RUURS ~ PAINTINGS BY ANDREW KISS

tundra

Tundra Books, an imprint of Penguin Random House Canada Young Readers, a Penguin Random House Company

Library and Archives Canada Cataloguing in Publication

Ruurs, Margriet, 1952-, author
          Wild babies / Margriet Ruurs ; illustrated by Andrew Kiss.

Issued in print format.
ISBN 978-0-88776-627-5 (hardcover).

QL763.R89   2003j591.3'9   C2002-904144-9

Published simultaneously in the United States of America by Tundra Books of Northern New York,
an imprint of Penguin Random House Canada Young Readers, a Penguin Random House Company

Library of Congress Control Number: 2002111645

Designed by Cindy Elisabeth Reichle
Typeset in Minion Pro by Tundra Books, Toronto
Printed and bound in China

www.penguinrandomhouse.ca

8   9   23   22

Penguin
Random House
tundra   TUNDRA BOOKS

To Myrtle, with thanks for looking after my wild babies.

— M.R.

To my son, Lee, and daughter, Rita, who were once my favorite babies.

— A.K.

Little bandits steal across the mossy roots, raccoon kits searching for berries.

A moose calf explores the forest on wobbly legs.

A sleek otter pup soaks up the summer sun. Go ahead, dive in the cool creek!

Downy goslings snuggle safely under Mama goose.

Skunk kits snuffle for food on the forest floor.

Mama bear takes her cubs for a romp in the alpine meadow.

Bright-eyed fox cubs will dash into their den if they sense any danger.

Mountain goat kids clamber up rocky slopes.

A fawn takes a nap in sun-dappled shadows.

Safe on Mama's back, a loon chick sails among the reeds.

Cougar cubs tumble and pounce, testing each other's strengths as they play.

Tiny wolf cubs open their eyes to the wild world.

~ LEGEND ~

What can you find in each painting?

RACCOON (page 4–5)

Can you find the robin's eggs in the branches? Do you see the moose's hind leg near the tree trunk? Do you see the word *moose* written on a mossy log?

When raccoon babies are about seven weeks old, their mother moves them away from the den they were born in. She carries them by the neck, just like a cat does with her kittens.

Raccoons are great climbers. They eat berries, roots, crayfish, and insects.

MOOSE (page 6–7)

Try to find the otter's tail in the creek on the right. Do you see the word *otter* on the tips of the grasses, in front of the moose? Can you find the frog on the rock by the river?

When a moose is first born, its mother keeps it hidden in shrubs or on an island. Within days, it can out swim a person!

Moose gain weight faster than any other animals in North America. An adult moose eats about twenty-five kilograms (55 lb) of twigs and leaves per day

in the summer. A moose can dive more than five meters (16 ft) for plants growing on the bottom of a pond. A long nose and flexible lips let it graze underwater.

OTTER (page 8–9)

Try to find the word *goose* in the branches near the hidden head of a goose. Can you see the turtle swimming?

Mother otters are excellent teachers. When the pups are two to three months old, the mother takes them on her back into the water. She dives under, slowly teaching them to swim on their own. When otters dive for fish, their nose and ears close up and become watertight. Otters are very playful. They slide down riverbanks, chase each other, and even throw rocks to dive for!

GOOSE (page 10–11)

Can you find the butterfly? Hidden just behind the grasses is the tail of a skunk. Do you see the word *skunk* under the goslings?

Geese fly in a V formation to help each other. By flying together their wings create an updraft, giving the flock a seventy percent greater flying range than if each bird flew on its own. Some geese spend the winter in Mexico and then fly all the way back to the Arctic to lay their eggs and hatch their goslings in spring. If one bird gets injured, two others stay with it until it can fly again.

SKUNK (page 12–13)

Do you spot the bear's paw on the top of a rock? You can also find the word *bear* near the top of the painting.

The Latin name for skunk is *mephitis*, meaning 'bad smell.' For safety, the skunk relies on its two scent glands, which can emit a yellowish oil with a terrible smell. Even the skunk itself hates it and tries not to use it unless absolutely necessary. Skunks are one of the most useful mammals around because of the huge number of insects they eat.

BEAR (page 14–15)

Try to find the pheasant in the tall, tall grass. Hidden, just behind the mother bear's hind leg is the word *fox*. Can you find it? Do you spot the fox's tail near a rock?

When bear cubs are born in their den during the winter, they are as long as a pencil. Human babies weigh twelve times more than baby black bears at birth!

Bear cubs grow up to be excellent runners and swimmers. Bears are omnivores: they use their claws to dig for roots and eat apples, fish, meat, insects, and plants.

FOX (page 16–17)

Do you see the leg of a mountain goat hidden between the birch trees? The word *goat* is written on the tree trunks. Can you find three foxes?

The fox is a small relative of the dog, coyote, and wolf. It is shy and very smart. Foxes have a litter of one to ten pups and make patient, playful parents. Both parents go out hunting and bring back food to their pups.

MOUNTAIN GOAT (page 18–19)

Do you see the word *deer* in the rock face? Try to find a fawn that is hidden among the rocks.

The mountain goat's hooves are like little suction cups. They prevent the snow white goats from slipping when they climb steep slopes. Mountain goats migrate up and down the mountains with the seasons.

DEER (page 20–21)

Can you find the loon hiding behind the bushes by the water? You can also find two loons that are about to take flight. Do you notice the word *loon* in the blue flowers?

Deer usually have twin babies. Within minutes of being born, a fawn gets up on its wobbly legs to drink its mother's milk. The spots on its back and the fact that it is odorless hide it from predators. The mother stays away from the baby, so she doesn't lead any enemies to it, and only returns to nurse it.

Antlers are bones with an internal blood supply and are covered in velvet. Only males grow antlers, which appear in early spring and drop off each winter.

LOON (page 22–23)

The word *cougar* is hidden in the trees. Do you see the cougar on the rocks across the water?

Loons are like little submarines. They can float, slowly sink, or quickly dive. Underwater loons can out swim a fish! They can stay underwater for more than five minutes. When these birds need to fly, they can only take off from water, not from land! Their call sounds like a strange, haunted cry.

COUGAR (page 24–25)

Do you see the wolf in the trees? Try to find the word *wolf* at the bottom of the hill.

The cougar is one of the largest members of the cat family and can stalk silently on padded feet, using sight and smell to hunt. When the cubs are born, the mother will not allow the male anywhere near. She nurses them for four to five weeks and teaches them to hunt. The cubs stay with their mother for about a year and a half. By that time the male cubs are bigger than their mother!

WOLF (page 26–27)

The wolf's coat adapts to the place where he lives. Arctic wolves are white, while the ones in southern forests have blackish brown coats. Wolves live in packs and have a well-developed social order.

Young wolves learn to hunt and how to behave in the social ranking through play. They talk to each other to warn or to encourage, by howling. The cubs are born in a whelping den. Once they start to move about, and when both parents want to go hunting, a member of the pack baby-sits the cubs. Wolves can run up to fifty kilometers per hour (32 mph)!

Do you see the new sapling pine tree? Pine trees are evergreens. Trees with leaves are called deciduous trees. Forests are vitally important to ensure shelter and food for many generations of wild babies to come.

What are the babies, males, females, and groups of animals called?

ANIMAL	BABY	MALE	FEMALE	GROUP
raccoon	kit	boar	sow	nursery
moose	calf	bull	cow	herd
otter	pup	male	female	family
goose	gosling	gander	goose	gaggle
skunk	kit	male	female	surfeit
bear	cub	boar	sow	sleuth
fox	cub	dog	vixen	leash
goat	kid	billy	nanny	herd
deer	fawn	buck	doe	herd
loon	chick	male	female	flock
cougar	kitten or cub	tom	queen	clutter
wolf	pup	dog	bitch	pack